The Pillars

4

Success

Stephen J. Palmer

Unless otherwise indicated, all Scripture quotations are taken from the *King James Version* of the Bible.

1st Edition

The Pillars 4 Success Copyright © 2014 by Stephen J. Palmer
Published by TPH Group, LLC
Stone Mountain, Georgia

Printed in the United States of America. All rights reserved under International Copyright Law. Contents and/or cover may not be reproduced in whole or in part in any form without the express written consent of the Publisher.

ISBN: 1505926912
ISBN-13: 978-1505926910

The Pillars Four Success

How to Turn Knowledge into Action and Action into Success!

STEPHEN J. PALMER

DEDICATION

I dedicate this book to my Father and Savior. For without Him we are nothing and with Him anything is possible. Thank you for helping me to be deliberately consistent, discipline and prepare for opportunities. May you be glorified in the lives that are changed from reading this book.

DAILY AFFIRMATIONS

I am **DELIBERATE**:
I live on purpose, for purpose, with purpose.

I am **CONSISTENT**:
I take progressive positive and profitable actions.

I am **DISCIPLINED**:
I do what must be done to accomplish that which I want to achieve.

I am **PREPARING FOR OPPORTUNITIES**:
I plan purposefully and prayerfully, counting all my cost with consideration on what I want to achieve.

"I pursue my success with persistence, making me poised and ready for whatever may come my way."

CONTENTS

Preface

Before You Read

1	Pillar One: Deliberate Actions	1
2	Pillar Two: Consistent	26
3	Pillar Three: Discipline	42
4	Pillar Four: Prepare For Opportunities	55
5	What Next: Your Turn	71
6	A Little Extra to Remember	75
	About the Author	79

PREFACE

I will never forget the words on August 31, 2007 that rang clear as a bell in my ear as I sat on the chair in my room after doing some reading and praying:

"You must be [Deliberate], Consistent, Disciplined, and Prepare for Opportunities if you want to have Success."

If you are like me and any of the millions of people that bought success books or the other several millions who contribute to the billion dollar self-help industry, you probably have heard everything there is to hear about becoming successful. If you have partaken in any of the countless seminars or read any of the myriad of books and articles on success, you undoubtedly received valuable information. But let me ask you: have you seen any major changes or showed any substantial progression? Did you practice for a week or maybe two, or even a month the lessons you learned only to eventually find that you went back to your earlier everyday routines? Were there so many different lessons, rules, and "need-to-know" information that you became so overwhelmed that you just said, "Forget about it"?

Chances are you are reading this book because you have a desire to be successful in whatever picture or manner that looks like to you. The problem (which I call opportunity) is that you have not been able to see that success, as of yet or maybe not as quickly as you would like. I have found that many people know how to be successful but lack the actions to implementing what they know. They suffer from one or two things: Paralysis of Analysis or Information Overload.

<u>Paralysis of Analysis</u> is when a person is over-thinking or analyzing a situation so much so that they waste all their time thinking and not doing anything at all.

<u>Information Overload</u> is when a person has so much information that they do not know where to begin or they are like a slow running computer that has run out of space so there is little to no action because of the overload.

In other words, it is not a problem of knowledge; it is a problem of application. How do you properly and effectively apply the lessons, book readings, and notes from the seminars into your life? Many people have the systems, the lessons, the understanding to get what they want in life; however they fail to apply what they have in the correct way in order to achieve their desired outcome. Consequently, if you are reading this book you are trying to unlock or find that missing link to why you have not seen the 'success' you want.

This book is intended to help you obtain the success you seek, sustain the success you obtained, and learn how to regain success through deliberate, consistent, and disciplined actions. I will practically show you how to apply everything you have learned and heard from the information you have gained through the countless hours of seminars, readings and money spent on your personal self-improvement.

What you have to do is strategically implement that knowledge using four simple, yet power applications I call *The Pillars Four Success*. These pillars are the foundation on which the principles of success (the knowledge you have learned) are built. Proverbs 24:3-4 puts it this way,

"It takes wisdom to build a house, and understanding to set it on a firm foundation; it takes knowledge to furnish its rooms with fine furniture and beautiful draperies." (MSG)

Knowledge only fills your rooms but does not build the house. You must build before you fill and this is when you will begin to see the success you want in your life.

My goal as you read this book is to give you more in use value than you have given in monetary value. To do so I will show you how to be deliberate in your actions, consistent in your behaviors, disciplined in your attitude and focused on preparation.

You have everything you need and everything it takes to succeed inside of you and I want to show you how to unlock what is inside. So, if you are ready, turn the page and let's get started.

BEFORE YOU READ

Why is it that you are not successful? Is it that you do not have enough knowledge or enough education? Is it because you do not have enough resources or money? Why are you not successful? Why are you not where you want to be in life? By no means am I trying to condemn you or talk you down. I am trying to invoke some real self-evaluation; some real internal thinking. Wallace D. Wattles concluded in his book, *The Science of Getting Rich*,

"Most people try to treat the symptoms in their lives and not the causes."

Your outward life is only a symptom to what your internal beliefs are. Therefore, let me pose the question another way, what do you believe when it comes to your success?

I will prove anybody wrong who believes that it only takes knowledge, education, money, or other resources to become successful. You can review the Forbes Billionaire List and find that there are countless stories, testimonies, and examples of individuals who have achieved high standards of success with having little or sometimes none of the stated factors above. These particular individuals did not have all the knowledge, they were not the most educated, they did not have the most money or they did not have all the resources.

What made them different? What set them apart from everyone else? In this book I want to show you how you can succeed. No matter what you have or do not have (at the moment). When it comes down to it, it is not about what you have on the outside as much as it is about who you are and what you possess on the inside. A powerful study about personal power says,

"You must *BE, DO* and then *HAVE*. In society we want to *HAVE, DO* and then *BE*."

To believe you must "have, do and be" is the wrong ideology. The fundamental application of successful living is:

You must first become, then as you become you do, and as you do you will begin to have that which you desire.

You are a success because you chose to be a success and take the deliberate, consistent, disciplined, prepared actions to do so. That is the bottom line. As I stated to you earlier, my number one goal for writing this book is to give you more in value than what you have given in monetary exchange. What this says is that I want you not just to have another book on your shelf to say that you have read it and gain nothing from the pages that you have read. I want you to take this book and apply it to your life and reap the rewards of the words written on the pages. In order to do this we must take the first preliminary step and make this book personal.

MAKE IT PERSONAL

I have found that through the years when I personalize items or activities, I tend to give more effort and take more responsibility because my name is tied to it. When you own something you tend to give it more attention, detail and time. You put forth genuine effort to maintain what you have acquired. Therefore, if you have not already done so, write your name on the front inside cover of the book and the back inside cover of the book. Also underneath your name on the front inside cover of the book, I want you to put the date of when you first started reading the book and whenever you complete the book I want you to put the date on the back inside cover. This will give you a specified timeline to track and evaluate what you have learned and monitor your progress as you read through the pages.

On the title page I deliberately put a blank line above the title so that you could write in your name. After you write in your name the title page should look comparable to the following example below, except of course, for the name: *Stephen J. Palmer's The Pillars Four Success*. After completing the above task, I want you to choose a pen and/or highlighter that you will only use for this book. These two items will be your tools for making notes and emphasizing particular points. It can be any color you choose or decide, but it will be the only pen and/or highlighter you will use on this book. (I found it quite easier to tie a rubber band around the book, pen and highlighter to keep it in place.)

GAIN AND GIVE

After you have selected your pen and/or highlighter I want you to grab a blank sheet of paper and draw a line directly down the middle of the page. On one side of the page I want you to write *Gain* and on the other side I want you to write *Give*. On the *Gain* side write down four (4) things you want to learn, know, accomplish and do after and while reading this book. On the *Give* side write down the 4 things you are willing to sacrifice in order to see what you want on the *Gain* side. Take your time and think about each section. See yourself giving and gaining what you have written down.

This is your book now, your time, your life, and frankly put, your moment. Value your life by investing whatever needs to be given to gain all that you set out to accomplish.

THE 6 INEVITABLE QUESTIONS

Finally, I intentionally structured the book to always answer what I like to call the "Six Inevitable Questions", who, what, when, where, how, and why. The "who" is defined as being you, the reader. To begin, you are responsible for reading the pages and taking the necessary steps to applying what you have read to your life. "What" is about the particular actions that need to take place. This is all about your 'to do list' and things you need to get done during and after you read. The "when" is about a particular time you will do the "what". "Where" talks about the specified areas that you need to establish the "what" in your life. And the "how" and "why" questions discuss the way or manner the "what" gets done and also defines the reason for doing the "what". Answering these questions allow you as the reader to elaborate on the information discussed and bring clarity to what you read.

So, Let's Get Started…

Pillar One:

DELIBERATE ACTIONS

"Anything can be achieved in small deliberate steps."
- Anonymous

There are three types of people in life:

1. People that let life happen

2. People that watch life happen

3. People that make life happen

People that "Let Life Happen", often do things just to do things. They have no real purpose or reason for their actions. They let whatever happens in life be the final say so and the only way things can be done. They hardly ever change and are often individuals filled with the infamous excuse: *"It is what it is, that is life."*

People that "Watch Life Happen" have no ambitions or goals for their life. They will often see other people achieving and accomplishing goals, yet have none for themselves. If they do set goals, chances are that they may have seen someone else do something and they try to do the same thing thinking that maybe they can be happy, but if they fail they say, *"oh well, I can't help that this happened."* After trying to accomplish a goal that has failed, these individuals become more like the people that let life happen and fool themselves into believing that if they let life happen, everything will be just "dandy, swell, and A- ok!"

The last category of people are the individuals in life who most people want to be like, envy, hope and wish to become. People that "Make Life Happen" have no excuse only actions that bring them closer to their goals and becoming successful. These people do little talking and more doing. They know that letting life happen or watching life happen is not living at all. They live their life with the motto:

"It is better to try and fail, than not to try at all."

If you are not deliberate with your life, someone else will be. To be deliberate is best defined as, *done with careful consideration, resolved upon, determine; studied, to reflect upon, slowly thinking and purposely selected.* Being deliberate answers the question: "Why do I do what I do?

DO YOU HAVE ACTION(S)

Success is a deliberate action. You do not just wake up one day and are successful. It involves careful consideration with a determined purpose. Successful people live on purpose, for purpose with a purpose. Nothing is done by accident or is coincidental. Ecclesiastes 3:17 puts it this way,

"…For there is a time there for every purpose and for every work." (NKJV)

Everything has a reason, a purpose for being. If you have no purpose you have empty actions and are just going through the motions. It is like running on a treadmill with your eyes closed, thinking you are heading somewhere, only to find when you open your eyes that you are in the same place. You are a person that let's life happen or watch life happen, but never makes life happen. You must have a purpose to why you do what you do. If you have no purpose you really have no life. When you don't have purpose to your actions it is like running on that treadmill thinking that you are going somewhere, when all you are doing is running in place staying in one location wasting time and energy. If you say you do not know what your purpose is consider the following adage:

"Your purpose in life is to find your purpose and give your whole heart and soul to it."
–Gautama Buddha

If you are unclear about what your purpose is, then your purpose is to find what your purpose is and pursue it. In other word: *"Make finding your purpose, your purpose if you are not sure what your purpose is."*

LOOK WITHIN

Everything you do starts internally before it is ever seen, manifested or externally received. A seed goes into the ground first and then grows outward. A bird grows in the egg and then hatches into the world. A mother carries a child for nine months inside the womb, before she gives birth. In each of these instances, there is a deliberate action that takes place before anything is ever seen externally. With that deliberate action there is a purpose whether it be to plant a flower with that seed, raise a bird that can soar from the egg, or have a child that can impact the world from the womb; success is deliberate and on purpose with an initial internal decision to become successful.

> **"Decide what you want, decide what you are willing to exchange for it.
> Establish your priorities and go to work."
> –H. L. Hunt**

MAKE A DECISION

One of my favorite authors and speakers, Jack Canfield author of *The Success Principles*, always states to his listeners the first step to becoming successful, one must:

"[You have to] first decide what you want."

Making a Decision involves a method I like to call "Intentional Progression". Intentional Progression as I define it simply means doing everything, on purpose, for purpose, with purpose with an intention to progress. It is similar to Newton's First Law: **"For every action there is an equal and opposite reaction."**

What you put out is what you get. Hence if you put nothing out, you get nothing back. It is just like seed time and harvest time and reaping what you sow, but in a manner in which you purposed.

PUT PURPOSE WITH YOUR ACTION

Tie a purpose to everything you do. This gives your actions and eventually your life a specified meaning. This is the way of life. All natural things are in a constant state of progression which is called the circle of life. You can choose to believe it or not, but I guarantee you see examples of this every single day. God made it this way **on purpose** (His Deliberate Actions), so that a cycle and a fortified system would be put into place for every living thing.

You put a seed inside the ground and that seed grows into a flower that flower produces more seeds, which produces more flowers while the initial flower we planted has already withered away. The bird hatches from the egg and embarks on the new journey of life, learning everything from flying to securing food reproduces of its own kind and breathes its last breath leaving the world. And as you might expect, you and I as homo sapiens are birth from our mothers; go through infancy stage progressing (maturing in our natural bodies) to the adult stage until we are eventually old enough to see wrinkles upon wrinkles of our skin and the sturdy pep we used to have in our step goes to a limp, slow slide and then we breathe our last breathe.

When you make a decision you are taking responsibility over your life and the results that you can control, this gives you the advantage. God just asks you to do your part and he will do his. Just like the seed, you cannot make a tree out of it, all you can do is plant it and God will take care of the rest. The easy part is up to you the hard part is up to God. Therefore the journey of success is only a decision away.

DEFINE YOUR PURPOSE

If life and in the example of nature automatically gives us this progression, it is wise for us to do in like manner and put a purpose on every action we take. You have to define a purpose to your success. Why is it that you want to see a particular outcome? Being deliberate means you have made a decision before you decide to act.

You must answer the "Why Questions" in your life. Why do you go to work? Why do you want to achieve this? Why does success look like this to you? Answering the 'whys' will help you along the journey which will inevitably get tough and trials will come (See Pillar 2 CONSITENCY); Understanding the purpose for doing something helps you to stay focused and eventually accomplish your plans.

> **"If you have a purpose in which you believe, there is no end to the amount of things you can accomplish."**
> **–Marian Anderson**

When you are deliberate you have made the choice to tie a purpose with your action which brings you a step closer to reaching your goals and becoming a success.

THE POWER OF CHOICE

CHOICE! Everything starts with a choice. Every day you wake up you are face with choices. Life is surrounded and built up or down by the choices you make. Choices come from your internal decisions, therefore, Life begins internally before it is ever seen or manifested externally. Thus everything you want to accomplish must begin within you before it can ever be received or seen outside of you.

Let's look back at the example the seed: a seed goes into the ground first and then grows in the hidden areas before it break out into the world. An even better example would be how you and I came into this world in our mother's womb. We were hidden beings developed and nurtured until we were fully ready and physically mature to be birthed. In the very beginning you do not see signs that a woman is pregnant. There may be symptoms but for most part, the pregnancy is unknown, hidden until things begin to change inside the woman's body that start showing on the outside of her body. The same is true when making choices. Others around you may not know why you make a particular choice or how you came about choosing a specific action, but the effects of your choice will start to show as you continue along in your life.

We have failures and successes based on the choices that we have made.

"Success is not a matter of chance, it is a matter of choice; it is not a thing to be waited for, it is a thing to be achieve."

−Samar Mansour

Choice is a powerful gift that many people neglect to use. In essence it is the only thing that belongs to you. Everything else in life is on loan from God. Choices, not chances determine whether or not you reach your desired outcome. Every day you do not decide to better your life, you are deciding to conform to the rhetorical, and unknown mishaps tomorrow will eventually bring. You must make a choice and decide what you want and be deliberate in your pursuit of it.

CLOSE YOUR EYES

What do you see when you close your eyes? (Go ahead take a moment to close your eyes). Is it pitch black? Is it dark? This darkness may appear to be nothing. However to the decided mind, it becomes an endless canvas to which you can create everything you wish and dream, right there in the delicate, powerful, and ever valuable instrument we call the mind—one of your greatest Treasuries of Life. Think of it this way. In Genesis 1:2 it says that,

"The earth was without form and an empty waste, and darkness was upon the face of the very great deep (Amplified)."

That is just like your mind sitting there nothing being formed in it, empty because you have not filled it, and being wasted because you are not using it. Using your mind is putting it work. Being deliberate in choosing what it is that you want and place it in your mind.

The next verse goes on to say,

> **"And God said, let there be light and there was light."**
> **Genesis 1:3 (Amplified)**

If you continue on you see that God made the world by creating things until everything He saw was "very good". What does that say to you? It says that you can create everything you want and desire, nevertheless you must make the choice on what it is that you desire. If you want something in life decide on it, create it and make it happen and make it good!

"INTERSECTION OF CHOICE"

When faced with particular decisions in my life, I tend to recall upon a story I once heard from a friend of mine name Coach Drew. He told me the following story:

My 18-year-old son was headed to college—ready to get out of the house and have the freedom to make his own choices and explore the world. I was excited to see him progress but I was concerned that his over zealousness could lead him to make poor choices, without thinking of the consequences. As I drove my son to his college dorm room, I was coming to a particular intersection that I thought would be a perfect opportunity to help him understand the power of making the right choices.

As I came to the intersection, I slowed the car down and pulled over to the nearest parking lot and parked the car. I asked my son to get out and follow me as we walked to the corner of the street out of the way of traffic, where the four way intersection sign was posted. I asked my son did he know which direction we needed to go to get to his college and he correctly pointed straight ahead in the direction we were previously driving and where you could clearly see the sign to his college campus. I then asked him to point in the direction of the where we once came, and again he correctly pointed to where we previous drove. Finally I asked him which route would be an alternative route to get to his campus to which he correctly pointed to the right.

I turned to the left in the direction that I never questioned him about and that he neither pointed. I told him that in that direction not too far down was one of the most poverty and crime infested locations in the city. He looked in astonishment. I assured him not to be worried but be reminded that each day he would be faced with a choice just like being at this intersection. If he want to excel and move ahead he would then go ahead in the direction of his college or turn to the right here which would take him through an alternative route but would still get him to his college. I then told him that if he felt like he could not make the right choice he could always go back to where he came but it would put him back where he once was and he would be not moving head.

Finally I told him that taking the other path toward the left would not only lead him away from the school and back from where we came but also lead him to poverty, crime, and possibly death. The choice to better your life is always in front of you. You choose whether you want to move ahead, go backwards or deviate from both. The choice is up to you.

We are all faced with the same kind of choices every day. Whether we will move ahead, go backwards or deviate all together. Your choices determine your outcome and without surprise your success. This reminds me of the last three lines of Robert Frost's 1920 poem "The Road Not Taken". In the last stanza it reads:

> **"Two roads diverged in a wood, and I—I took the one less traveled by, and that has made all the difference."**

This depiction of choice leads to great satisfaction for Frost. Choosing to decide on the road was the most difficult, but after he decided and made his choice, he then could become deliberate in his steps to support his present actions, future path and that determined his destination.

DETERMINE YOUR PURPOSE

"The secret of getting ahead is getting started…"
—Mark Twain

I have discovered that it is a lot easier to be deliberate when you have a purpose. Having a purpose is like paving a concrete path in an unmarked, overgrown terrain. Though things may look dismal or show some difficulty you can get through it because you have a marked out path to help you determine where to go, where to turn and how to get to your destination. Purpose is birth from a desire. A desire comes from a need. What are your needs? Needs are not just the day-to-day things such as more money, a bigger house, or any of the external things. When I talk of needs I am talking of deep concerns, issues that bother you in life or that you want to see changed. What burdens you? What causes you to get up every morning or stay up all night? What is it in your life or that is not in your life that you want to get rid of or obtain? Once you determine your need you have done half the work of defining the 'what' before you can determine the why.

BE SPECIFIC

Specify exactly what it is you desire. Make it clear,

concise, and so plain that if you had to write it out or draw a picture you could tell precisely what it is in great detail. If you and I were standing in the middle of a garden filled with hundreds upon hundreds of flowers and I say "go pick that flower." You would probably ask me, "What flower are you talking about?" It is not that you do not know what a flower is or where it is. You just have many options in front of you. In order to know which one I want I need to be more specific in my description. Now, if I say go pick the tall yellow flower with a brown center, you would be able to more easily find it and determine what it is that I wanted. Life is the same way. Success can be many different things to different people. However, in order for you to know what path to pave or what you desire to see, you have to make your purpose clear.

WHAT IS YOUR MISSION

A Mission is a summary that answers the question of "Why" you do what you do. Every move you make must have purpose. There must be a reason why you do what you do. Every step you make and every action you take must have a purpose to help keep you grounded and focused on your journey to your destination. Each day you are walking on the paths of life that inevitably shape your future. Therefore, nothing that you do is trivial and should not be done without a specific, defined and determined purpose.

ESTABLISH YOUR PLAN

"Never begin the day until it is finished on paper."
−Jim Rohn

Never start a day you have not finished. Tie a purposeful plan to your 24 hour day. Do not let the day simply go by and the time slip away into another day. Make each day count by establishing plans that are moving you in the direction of your destination. General S. Patton transcribed:

"A good plan today is better than
a perfect plan tomorrow."

And he would know. He received 25 different decorated medals from his countless times at war. General S. Patton understood that today, right now is the best time to plan for the future, not waiting until tomorrow to do so. Tomorrow is not promised but right now is! Statistically speaking, "one out of every one person will die". You do not know if tomorrow will be your day. Waiting for tomorrow wastes another day in your life to move you closer to you destination. Many people make the excuse that they want to wait on 'one day' and 'someday'. Neither of these days are on the calendar nor fall on the days of the week. One day never happens and someday never comes. You must make a conscious effort to plan today, right now; not letting procrastination or laziness stop you from moving forward.

PLANS AND PURPOSE

Plans are important on your journey to your destination because plans have purpose tied to them.

> **"Surely, as I have planned, so it will be, and as I have purposed, so it will happen."**
> **—Isaiah 14:24 (NIV)**

You do not wait for everything to be in order or to have more resources before you start to plan, you do it now! When you fail to plan, you plan to fail. What are your plans for succeeding? What will you *deliberately* do in order to have what you desire and purpose for your life? Do you even have a plan? If God has to make plans for His purposes, what makes you think that you and I do not have too? You must create your purpose and establish the plan(s) for seeing that purpose come about. Planning helps you to eliminate stress, focus through difficult times, and allows you to evaluate your progression or lack thereof. If you were to attend a mandatory formal dinner and you did not have anything to wear, would you not deliberately go out and find the appropriate attire? Imagine you go out to a store and the sales person asks, "Can I help you"? Because you have a purpose and a planned time for what you are looking for, you can easily explain to the sales person what you need and when you need it. In return the sales person can assist you with great ease and maybe even add some helpful suggestions to help you accomplish your goal. Life works in a similar way. Each of us has an 'event' which represents where you desire to be and go in life. We have to plan our steps accordingly to see that plan through every step of the way. And God wants to assist you in achieving your purpose, but you have to establish the plans.

> **"A person plans his way, but he Lord directs his steps."**
> **Proverbs 16:9 (ISV)**

If you do not plan your ways the Lord cannot direct your path. You can have all the dreams and desires to become successful, but if you have not created your plans you will not only limited how far you can go [if anywhere] but also limited God's Hand by directing your steps to reach your destination.

WRITE IT DOWN

I constantly hear people say that they have a plan, but when I ask them where is it they tell me: "it's in my head." A plan is not a plan until it is written down. When you plan you create a map for where you want to go and what you have to do to get there. No matter how small or large your plan is, it needs to be written down. I have often heard my mentors say:

"A short pencil is better than a long memory."

This is to say, it is better to have things written down instead of just having them in your head. It is okay for you to have your plans in your head if you have already written them down. Here are four benefits for writing down your plans:

1. You can create a backup version of your plans other than just keeping them in your head where things can be forgotten.

2. You now have a physical tangible document that can be stored away and valued.

3. You can read them aloud and can easily make changes as needed.

4. You can show it to others and make copies as needed to those who can help you accomplish your plans.

Writing your plans down give you an advantage of seeing your plans outside of your mind and creating a tangible document that you can share with yourself by reading aloud or with those who can help you reach your destination.

WORK THE PLAN

> **"You have to plan the work,
> then work the plan."
> —Bishop Dale C. Bronner**

Once you have decided where you want to go; determined your purpose through planning and written down your plans, you must then work your plans. This takes diligence and a disciplined attitude (See Pillar 3: DISCIPLINE). However what is clear is that you must plan first so that you can have something in which to work on. Planning is purposeful and strategic in nature.

SILVER PLATTER

It is sad to see that a lot of people live with what I call the "Silver Platter Mentality". This mentality is detrimental to your success due to the idea that: just because you know something or have a particular look, you think that somebody is going to bring what you want to you. You think that what you desire is going to fall right into your lap; you are going to automatically meet the right people, be in the right place and get what you desire, just because. Just because something did not happen, or just because you want something to happen, you think it will happen. This is far from the truth and reality alike. You do not get what you want in life, you get what you plan and prepare for. But many people are not willing to plan for what they want and others are not willing to prepare the plans (See Pillar 4: Preparing for Opportunities).

We cannot live our lives in an unintentional way. Just because you spent hundreds of dollars on seminars, books, CDs, and logged hours upon hours in self-help improvement, or even because your mother, father, brother, sister, cousin, or friend achieved their goals does not mean you will achieve yours. You have the knowledge and that is good. By no means am I demeaning the knowledge you have learned throughout the years and even now reading this book. What I want to register within your subconscious and eventually into your way of life is that knowledge, alone does not make you successful. It is the action(s) of that knowledge that will make you successful. When you deliberately make a decision, when you deliberately determine your purpose, and strategically plan from the knowledge you have gained you have then taken the proper steps to lay the foundation for your successful life.

INSPECT WHAT YOU EXPECT

As a Deputy Sheriff I worked inside the county jail where we had many incidents and occasions of testing through planning and the lack there of. Often in our roll call meetings one of the Chief Deputies would get up and rehearse the phrase, he had said the night before and the night before that:

"Inspect what you expect!"

The act of being deliberate is looking into your life and measuring your progressions and eliminating your hindrances. This is called inspection. Whenever you ladies or gentlemen go to the salon or the barbershop, you tell them what you want and after they are finished and even at times while they are working, they will show you a mirror to inspect what you said you wanted. Inspecting what you expect is all about self-evaluation. We are all human and we will have "human moments"; when we make mistakes or simply neglect to do some things. This is why it is very important to evaluate your plan. If I asked you to write down as many things you know that you need to do to accomplish your goals or obtain the success you seek, you could probably think of a million things you know you could do to obtain what you desire. Likewise, if I asked you to write down why you "think" you could not obtain success you more than likely could name many reasons as well. Hence, what we call self-evaluation. An easy way to evaluate your plan and life in general, would be to answer the following three questions:

1. What should I stop doing?
2. What should I start doing?
3. What do I need to continue doing?
4. What must I improve on?

The way this works is you look at the 'million things' you know you should be doing based on the countless hours and lessons from the seminars, books, and lessons you have learned throughout the years. If you are not doing something start to do what you know needs to be done. If you have put something else in place of the task that you know you need to start doing, stop doing it and replace it what you should start doing. Successful people deliberately evaluate the plans in their life to ensure they are on the right path to achieving their desired outcome.

HAVE DO BE or BE DO HAVE.

> **"What you get by achieving your goals is not as important as what you become by achieving your goals."**
> **—Zig Ziglar**

Too many times we try to have things and acquire

objects or possessions thinking that they will help us to be better or become better. It is this ideology that has helped to create the debt crisis and makes many credit card companies fortunes off of the misfortunes, better yet, misunderstanding of others. You should never put your focus on trying to have things. Instead, "Be" the person that deserves to have the things. The old adage says it best, "Do not put the cart before the horse." Benjamin Franklin observed it this way,

**"One day is worth two tomorrows;
what I am to be I am now becoming.**

What you want to be, you must be every single day because each day you live and the things you do or choose not to do affect your tomorrow(s). You will not always 'have' now, but you can always 'be' now. You do not need to wait until you get more education, money, a better job, a car, or anything of that sort. Make the deliberate conscious decision to be right now what you want. Start in the most valuable God given tool, instrument, and world profound gift, which is your mind. Put away the someday, one day, and the maybe. Someday and one day are not on the calendar and May is a month, but not Maybe! Right now is the opportune and best time you have. All you really do have is right now, because tomorrow is not promised. But when you set deliberate actions to make a decision, determine your purpose, and establish your plan, you are giving your body, your mind, and your very being a reason to live on.

YOU ARE THE BOTTOM LINE

**"You must take personal responsibility. You cannot change the circumstances, the seasons, or the wind, but you can change yourself.
That is the something you have charge of."
−Jim Rohn**

The bottom line is that only you, no one else; not your parents, friends, environment, or government is responsible for you. You create the limitations and barriers in your life. The excuses you make, the nonchalant and lazy attitude(s) have formed the bars and cells that have jailed you in. You have the key to unlocking your full potential. Being deliberate requires you to take action. Decide that you will do what it takes to be responsible for your life. Choose to do what it takes to see your goals accomplished.

Remember this, there is nothing wrong with going slow or taking your journey one day at a time. Honestly, that is all you can do. There is something wrong with letting life just happen. And not doing anything at all. That is why you first have to establish a deliberate choice and plan. You do not control whether or not you wake up, however you can and must decide that if you want to be successful, you will do all you can do today! John Wooden, one of the most prolific coaches and NCAA Hall of Famer eloquently put it this way,

"Make everyday a masterpiece."

Be deliberate in creating the life, the days, the hours, the minutes, and seconds you want to see in your life. Be deliberate in your actions to become successful.

THE 6 INEVITABLE QUESTIONS

I Must Deliberately live on purpose, for purpose and with purpose.

1. Whose purpose do I pursue? (Is this really my purpose or some other person's dream)?

2. What is my purpose (goal, destination, or objective) that I am pursuing?

3. When do I want to accomplish my purpose (goal, destination, or objective)?

4. Where will my purpose (goal, destination, or objective) take me or allow me to do or have?

5. Based on what I have read thus far, how will I accomplish my purpose (goal, destination, or objective)?

6. Why do I want to pursue this purpose in my life?

Pillar Two:

CONSISTENCY

"There is no shortcut to winning and success. There is only getting started and sticking to it."
- Anonymous

By far this is one of the most difficult of the Four Pillars for people to live out. Not only does it require you to be deliberate in every action, but you must continually do the necessary actions day in and day out no matter the current outlook, emotions, uncontrollable setbacks, feelings or others, etc. The outcome is what you focus on, but the outlook can become dismal, harsh, seem hopeless, asinine, and unrealistic; however you have to keep doing it.

"We walk by faith not by sight."

II Corinthians 5:7 (NKJV)

Allow your dream, the picture of your desired outcome and success keep you motivated. Do not be a start-and-stop-junky. A start-and-stop-junky is a person who has a lot of enthusiasm and the attitude not to quit in the beginning, but phases out and eventually stops then starts over again. My question is, why did you stop? What caused you to leave the path of success? Is your desired destination really worth it? If so, why did you stop? Starting and stopping your progress is like taking one of those 5 hours energy drinks and getting this burst of energy, but no consistency so you eventually crash, just to take another one. It does no good to have energy and no continual action for that energy, just like it does no good to start and stop your deliberate actions that lead you to your destination.

ASK YOURSELF WHY

You must ask yourself why you are not consistent. Who is hindering you from your desired outcome? What is taking up your time, money, and resources? You should have a daily regimen that should be congruent with the plans you established beforehand. Do not ever let up because there is a power that comes with your consistency. Results come from a deliberate consistent behavior that you do day in and day out. If you plan on being successful you can never let up just because it gets tough, hard or unbearable. Consistency is a form of perseverance. When I think of this concept I think of the word 'Kaizen. This is the Japanese word for 'improvement', or change for the better. The philosophy behind this word focuses upon the continuous improvement of any particular process. It is a daily process whose purpose is to nurture and to continue. What daily progression are you making on your journey to your destination? Are you continually improving from the day before or are you finding that you are phasing out?

ALLOW FOR TIME

> **"Lost time is never found again"**
> **−Benjamin Franklin**

As with anything worth having, there is a process involved. This process without a doubt, involves time. Time is a great gift if used correctly. Time is a gauge for evaluation to show you where you have improved or where you need improvement. It is valuable in many ways and consistent in all ways. There is no such thing as 'free time'. Time is not free, it costs either hours, minutes, or seconds. Whichever denominations of the three you give make up the currency of life. Therefore you have to plan your days and consistently stick with the plans so as not to waste your life. Time is a lot easier to handle when you have laid the plans and determined your purpose for your desired outcome. When you know your destination, the journey tends to be a lot less hectic, but nevertheless it does take time.

Think of a Chef that is baking a cake. The cake is prepared, placed in the oven and then has to sit in the oven until it is fully cooked and ready. If it comes out before hand, it is undone and the chef has no use for it so it will be discarded. If it comes out too late it will be overcooked and no one really wants to eat a burnt cake. You are like that cake and God is our master chef. How silly would it be for the cake to knock on the oven door and tell the chef that it is ready? You cannot control time, but you can choose to control your timing.

TIMING

Timing is about regulating your actions, or remarks in relation to what is happening to you so that you can get the best results. Timing involves having a focused outlook and a strategic plan. Timing is important on your journey because it requires you to utilize both the time that you have been given and the knowledge that you know. Timing is about answer the "when" and "how" questions. When will you reach your destination, but also how will you get there is all encompassed in how you utilize your time.

Let's say that you wanted to plant an orange tree. You acquire the knowledge and learn the lessons of how to plant a fruitful orange tree. You even get the "Orange Tree for Dummies First Edition" book and read through it to be sure you are taking the proper steps. So, you have set through these lessons, taken good notes, read the book and are ready to purchase your seeds. So you follow the advice of the book and purchase your seeds from a nearby successful farmer and you are ready to grow that orange tree! You put on your overalls, tie your bandanna around your neck, tie your shoes, grab your shovel, the seeds and proceed to walk outside, only to find that it is snowing.

Now you have spent all this time reading, learning, studying, and spending money on the seeds, shovel, and overalls, just to walk outside and realize that it is snowing. The issue is not that you do not know how to plant the seeds, or that you do not have seeds to plant. The issue is the timing. You want to plant but the weather is not conducive at the moment to plant an orange tree. In all reality, you can go out in the falling snow to plant your seed or put it in the ground, but eventually because of the weather that seed will not grow and may eventually die, all because the timing is not right. This is why it is important to make sure that your actions are not only consistent but that they are made during the proper time. Just like that orange tree seed; if you choose to take action at the wrong time, you could not only hurt your progress but delay your journey to success temporarily or even permanently depending on the actions taken.

PATIENCE IS A STRATEGY

Along with time on the journey of success, you must master the art of patience. I said, "Art" because patience is created in your life through time and the test, trials, and obstacles that you are sure to face. Patience is not just a virtue, it is a strategy. It is a tactic to teach you to stay consistent in your behavior no matter what you face. Do not just go through life, grow through life. James 1:4 makes it clear by stating,

"Let patience have its perfect work, that you may be perfect and complete, lacking nothing."
(NKJV)

Patience is producing perfection in you. It is strategically making you better as you go along the journey of success. However, do not be mistaken, patience is work. We live in an age/society of "Now, Right Now, and Already" minded people. We believe that everything should be given to us now. Then when we do not get it, we try to demand things, right now and after the right now does not happen we fashion our minds to think that what we want should have already come. It is silly and juvenile to think that things in life are going to happen instantaneously. If you really think about it, even 'instant popcorn' takes two to three minutes to make. The point of the matter is, you must be patience. It is a part of the journey. Patience does not mean you sit and twiddle your thumbs and whistle the time away. No, it means you consistently work out what needs to be worked on, sharpening your gifts and talents, sticking to your plans and develop along the way until you reach your destination. W. Edwards Deming believed,

"There must be consistency in direction."

If you are headed somewhere, which you are (your destination), you must stay consistent in that direction. Improve upon what you learned and already know. Practice your gifts and sharpen your skills in the areas that you know will help you reach your destination and that you know you will need along the way. Patience gives you time to prepare yourself and to make the proper timing, but you must be consistent in your pursuit.

THE UGLY DISEASE

As you stay consistent, you will develop a regimen and repetitions for doing certain things. In doing so, if you are not careful, and ugly disease that can hinder your journey and destroy your success can creep in. This ugly disease is called: Complacency!

> **"Complacency is a continuous struggle we all have to fight."**
> **—Jack Nicklaus**

You must be careful not to fall into complacency. Complacency takes place when you lose sight of the where and what you are going after. When you lose sight of these things become rhetorical, mundane, and the enthusiasm goes out the door along with your consistency. Complacency is dangerous because your mind, intellect and focus is really not into what you are doing. You are just going through the motions, moving, but not in a way that is improving and stretching you.

To defeat complacency you must be attentive and alert to areas where you find yourself just going through motions and not really thinking about what you are doing. If you subconscious is running the show, then you have to immediately awaken your conscious mind so that complacency will not find itself on your path.

> **"Never get too comfortable, always challenge yourself. Comfort oftentimes creates conditions for complacency."**
> **—Unknown**

If you have to change things up, but do not stop. Challenge yourself with new tasks and deviate from the normal routine. If you are in a particular space, go somewhere new. Do whatever you can to keep your mind alert and heart focused on your destination to reach your success.

THE TEST, TRIAL AND OBSTACLE

Have you ever set a goal or said that you would do something and it seems like everything comes against you or tries to stop what you said. It may be that you just got lazy and did not do it or that you had so much opposition that you neglected your task and let it alone. You must understand that every commitment you make will be tested.

Please understand that a faith walk is a battle that can tire you out and for the non-committed, non-deliberate, and weak minded it will crush you and cause you to quit. You have to

> **"Fight the good fight of faith..."**
> **—I Timothy 6:12 (NKJV).**

Though it is a fight, it is a good fight you are fighting, one that will strengthen you and get you closer and closer to your desired success. The very goal, dream, and success you look for will test you, beat you, try you, and break you down until it comes to pass. Psalm 105:19 said it like this talking about Joseph,

"Until the time that his word came to pass, the word of the Lord test [refined] him."
—Psalm 105:19 (NASB).

The test, trials, and obstacles you go through are all a part of the process to your journey of success. This is the order and how the economy of success works. You must toil the soil to reap the oil. You must be willing to give your deliberate, consistent actions everything you got.

Think of it through this quote,

"Give, and it will be given to you: good measure, pressed down, shaken together, and running over will be put you're your bosom.
For with the same measure that you use, it will be measured back to you."
(Luke 6:38 NKJV)

If that does not sound like a tussle or a fight I do not know what does. First you will receive a good measure which is a good amount of force that will be pressed down (something pressing down on top of you), then getting shaken up (together with your dream) and finally running over (spilled out). That is a lot of pressure and friction coming your way. But it has to take place in order for you to get back what you are wanting. Even so, be encouraged through this because what seems like resistance, pressure and hard efforts is actually a sign and indication that you are on the right path to accomplishing your desire outcome.

HOW LONG, NOT LONG

No matter what, you must make a resolve to be consistent, never quitting or letting up on your plans. During the Civil Rights Movement, Dr. Martin Luther King Jr. and many other unsung heroes and world changers faced countless gestures, actions, and words against their noble and divinely inspired pursuits of equality for all men. Dr. King addressed an enthused crowd on March 25, 1965 in Montgomery Alabama with a speech entitled *Our God is Marching On!* Near the end of his speech he poised a question that many people during that time were asking, *"How long will it take?"* I know that you may be wondering the same thing pertaining to this journey of success and going through the tests, trials and obstacles. Just as Dr.

King stated in that speech I will say,

"However difficult the moment, however frustrating the hour, it will not be long…"

Hold true to know that you will make it through and will be better off in the end because you endured the development that came with each test, trial, and/or obstacle you faced. There is true power in your consistency. A single drop of rain has no real power, but as each new drop of rain comes consistently steady one by one it can create a flooding or a powerful natural occurrence. The four seasons change each year without hesitation consistently bringing winter, spring, summer, and fall. Moreover with each new opportunity for life, occurs a natural replenishment and you are equally the same.

"Success is to be measured not so much by the position that one has reached in life, as by the obstacles which he has overcome."
−Booker T. Washington

Always commit to memory that the struggle is bringing your desired outcome. It is there to test you (get you ready), and then it is there to uncover the success, hidden away in the problems or frustrations you have. Make a resolve that you will not quit and God will never fail you. You will see your dream, your success, and your desired outcome all the way through until it becomes a reality. Romans 5:3-4 puts it this way,

"We also have joy with our troubles, because we know that these troubles produce patience. And patience produces character, and character produces hope. And this hope will never disappoint us..."

Your troubles (tests, trials, and obstacles) are producing the character that you need in order to succeed. They (tests, trials, and obstacles) are there to help better you along your journey to your desired outcome of success. You will make it and you will win. You do not lose because you do not quit. Always keep in mind that tests have a time frame, trials have an expiration date, and obstacles have a course with a finish. This means that all this adversity and (what seems to be) opposition have an end, but your consistency should not. See your dream through to the end of each test, trial and obstacle.

CONSISTENCY NEVER QUITS

A person of consistency becomes the mission, vision, dream or goal. They never waver despite what occurs. Likewise, you must embody your dream and become the success you seek. Do not let what happens around you or to you destroy what is in you. Let each setback become a setup for your success. Let each delay turn into a desire to keep moving forward. Use whatever you face to make you stronger, better, wiser and stepping block on your journey. Never forget that what *you want to be you have to be every single day.* Become all that you seek on the journey and heed the words of James,

"Count it all joy when you fall into various trials, knowing that the testing of your faith produces patience; but let patience have its perfect work, that you may be perfect and complete, lacking nothing."
− James 1:2-4

Keep going, keep growing, and keep sowing. Never quit, and never give up. Push through the difficulties, because on the on the other side of your troubles, you will have your desired outcome. Consistency is really about creating a system in your life that effectively implements the plans you established in order for you to reach your desired outcome. Since you are heading in the direction of success you must start today, and continue on to each tomorrow.

THE 6 INEVITABLE QUESTIONS

I Consistently take progressive, positive, and profitable actions.

1. Whose actions do I follow? (Do I have a good role model or mentor that I am following in their footsteps?)

2. What actions do I take toward becoming successful?

3. When do I need to start making my progressive, positive and profitable actions?

4. Where do my actions currently take me? (Are they progressive, positive or profitable)?

5. How will these actions help me become successful?

6. Why are these progressive, positive and profitable actions needed to be successful?

Pillar Three:

DISCIPLINE

> "It is one of the strange ironies of this strange life that those who work the hardest, who subject themselves to the strictest discipline, who give up certain pleasurable things in order to achieve a goal, are the happiest men."
> - Brutus Hamilton

A person of discipline has a greater chance of reaching their destination and obtaining success. They do not let the issues of life hinder them from following instructions and staying on their desired path. Though times may get hard, situations may become uncomfortable and issues will arise, they press each day until they reach their desired outcome.

TWO PAINS IN LIFE

"There are two pains in life. The pain of discipline and the pain of regret."
—Jim Rohn

The pain is of discipline is temporary, it only last for so long. The pain of regret can last for the rest of your life. You eventually become accustomed to the routine and the pain so you get acclimated to it and are able to handle it better than when you first begin. At first you did not like having to do the work and sacrifice things that you enjoy in order to get what you love. Usually the first steps in discipline are the most painful. Sometimes that pain can last days, weeks or even months, but it will eventually become just another feeling that you are able to handle if you stick with it. How you handle pain depends on your tolerance for it.

DANGERS OF INDOLENCE

Are you an indolent person? Indolent means that you purposely avoid pain. There are some people who are so indolent that they almost become like hermits. They never go anywhere or do anything because they know in some way, shape or form there may be some sort of pain. People who are like this avoid pain, but become lazy and fearful people who, you guessed it, never become successful. They literally scurry through life like a squirrel, who at the first sound they run off. They live in a state of paranoia, looking over their shoulder in fear; constantly dodging activities and various involvements in everyday living that they have end of having no life. Maybe you know someone like this or maybe you are this way. Whatever the case, you want to avoid being around this person or being like this person. Indolent people invite fear and laziness into their life. Fear and laziness are poisons and prisons to your success. If you allow fear to creep into your life, it will begin to poison your ambitions, weaken your drive and eventually kill your dream. You have to combat this fear with action.

PUSH BEYOND THE PAIN

I will never forget the time I was teaching my nephew how to ride his new bicycle. He was excited to go outside and try out his brand new BMX bike with all the new features. I put his helmet on and explained to him how to use the brakes found on each handle. His eagerness was apparent because before I could get the last word out of my mouth he was gone! He rode up the hills and down the hill; to the right and to the left. It brought joy to see how much fun he was having until he turned into our driveway and came crashing down off the bike. You see, this bike was taller than he was and he was used to dragging his feed on the ground to stop. When he was unable to do that he came crashing to the pavement with the bike following closely behind. Before he could start to cry, I ran over to him, dusted him off, and made sure he was not severely hurt and put him right back on the bike with a fanatic cheer: "KEEP RIDING, KEEP GOING AND HAVE FUN!"

You may think that what I did was inconsiderate and a bit abrasive. On the contrary. I knew from my experiences of learning to ride that you will fall down and sometimes you will fall really hard. Nevertheless, if you do not get up when you fall, no matter how hard, the pain will set in but more dangerous than the pain, the fear of getting back on would come in. Believe it or not, this is how most phobias are created. People have a bad traumatic experience and instead of getting back up and pushing through the pain to try again, they are left with the pain and fear of what took place, which causes them never to try that activity, action or encounter again.

FACE THE FEAR

Do not allow fear from failure, pain or from any person or thing stop you from being deliberate, consistent and discipline on your journey to your destination. Do not give fear any room in your thinking, feelings or actions. This is my whole reasoning behind immediately picking up my nephew after he fell down and before he could start to cry. I made sure that he did not give fear or any immediate pain the opportunity to stop him from a future or present progression. I wanted him to try again, not with the memory of the pain, but with the memory of the fun, knowing that he could do it. In the same way, you cannot expect to have success in your life if you do not try, try, and try again!

I know you are thinking: "what if I already have allowed fear to set in because of a past failure; a door closed in your face, your idea was rejected or you could not get past a certain point?" To you I would say, "GREAT"! You have learned what does not work and who is not interested. Now you can learn from those experiences to help you as you continue to move forward to your destination. It is a known fact that most people who are afraid of a particular task or person will avoid them. They will not involve themselves or associate with something or someone that they have an apparent fear of. Even if that task or person is something or someone that can help better their life, they will make excuses of why they should not work on a particular task and be around that person, no matter how beneficial it might be. This fear creates a prison of laziness and apathy. This person could very well excel in other areas, but here in the area where their fear exists they allow it to make them a prisoner to mediocre self-loathing, lazy and unproductive behaviors. They never go beyond a certain point in their life and they never will until they break free of the prison whose bars are made of laziness and the walls are made of their fears. Whatever fear is holding you back, whatever pain has caused you to stop moving forward, get rid of it so that you can have the success you want and deserve.

HAVE SOME FAITH

I am a man of faith, so I impart my faith to you. I am not a religious man, but a man with a relationship with God. I undoubtedly believe that

> **"God's unlimited power can be added to your human limited will power, to give you a divine discipline to achieve what you need internally and externally."**

Without self-control a person has little ability to receive the blessings of God and accomplish their desired outcome. Do not get bitter over things that happen or the pain of discipline, get better. Discipline is not about what happens to you it is about what you make happen. There will be times you will have to keep pushing, through the pain, the agony, and complete stress. However, if you endure you will overcome. You will see your desired outcome. In Psalm 15 the author speaks about who is the individual that can reach their desired destination. He goes on to answer the his own question in the latter half of the verse by saying,

> **"The one who makes a promise and does not break it, even though he is hurt by it."**
> **—Psalm 15:4 (GW)**

GROWTH AND DEVELOPMENT

It is your duty and responsibility to take care of your business; to seize and take advantage of the opportunities in your life and to do what must be done to grow and develop. In order to be able to seize opportunities and to allow for growth and development, you must be disciplined. Discipline is about development. You can always find ways to grow and develop, no matter where you are. Think of the flower that grows in the crack of the cement. Where others may see a problem, difficulty, frustration, or mistake the flower sees room to grow. You do not see any grass or other flowers around. Yet it still grows. You must be the same way. Never allow the terrain or your environment (where you are) to determine how you will or if you will grow. It is never about where you are it is always about what you have within you (who you are). Discipline reveals what has been in you all along. Therefore, who you are is greater than where you are!

WORK A BLESSING IN DISGUISE

**"Thou, Oh God, doth sell to us all good things at the price of labor.
Work is the seed from which grows all good things you hope for.
A man who's afraid of hard work better be brave enough to accept poverty".
Leonardo DaVinci**

Hard work, great sacrifice, and the foregoing of immediate gratification are all a part of being disciplined. No one is going to give you something just because you are a certain race, age, denomination, or any other difference. You have to work hard and even harder to pursue what you want and reach your desired outcome. Do not be deceived, you must work each and every day because it is your duty and responsibility if you want to succeed. In Genesis 2:2, on the seventh day God ended His **work** which he had done, and He rested on the seventh day from all His **work** which He had done. If God, the maker of heaven and earth had to work, what makes you think that you do not have to? The work you do is really a blessing for you. The work you do is equivalent to the sunlight and rain for a growing seed. At times it gets hot, cold, or wet, however, all that you go through is helping you grow and reach your desired outcome. Consequently, you can also be the hindrance and limitation to your own success if you choose not to work. Any kind of growth or success requires discipline and that discipline is work.

COUNT THE COST

Inevitably, time and pain are a part of the cost to becoming successful. The process can be daunting, tough, filled with issues that cause your emotions to go up and down and all over the place. The process can look like you will never get to where you want to go and the pain can become so unbearable. If you know it cost your time and some pain, you must learn to use time and grow a tolerance for pain. Discipline builds your tolerance and strengthens your ability handle the journey of success.

PAY THE COST

You know your destination, you know the cost, so now pay it. Truthfully speaking, on the journey to success the cost will be a lot more than you thought or calculated, but it is still small compared to the reward of accomplishing your goals. When setbacks, roadblocks and unforeseen things happen do not become discouraged or throw in the towel. Never stop pursuing your dream, climbing up or moving forward to reach your destination. Okay, things may have gotten delayed and did not go exactly like you planned. However, delay is not denial and unplanned circumstances are not derailments on your journey. The only way you could deny or derail yourself is by quitting. Being disciplined is not denial; it is just a strategic delay. Self-discipline is the ability to do what you should do when you should do it because you ought to do it. If you are to succeed it is up to you to pay the cost to do what it takes. Keep in mind that pain is temporary, and the feeling of knowing you reached your desired outcome lasts forever. Bruce Lee put it this way,

"There are no limits. There are plateaus, but you must not stay there, you must go beyond them. If it kills you, it kills you. A man must constantly exceed his level."

You must always strive to be better and do more.

FINISH WHAT YOU START

If you allow the uncalculated cost or unforeseen circumstances to stop you, then your destination, dream or goals are not worth it. When asked, "How can I make my life a success", Henry Ford would reply,

"If you start something, finish it!"

You must be disciplined enough to focus and finish what you start. Never stop when you are tired or frustrated, only stop when you are finished. After the thrill is gone, the initial excitement and enthusiasm have fizzled away, what do you do? Do you quit and later on beat yourself up because you quit? Discipline is about mastering yourself and not giving in to the hindrances or the distractions that try to stop you from accomplishing your desired outcome. It may be hard, things may get difficult—It may be frustrating and at times feel unbearable, but not one time will it be impossible.

Do not be like those people who think that just because they have determined their destination, started on their journey and even begin to pay the cost that they will not face trouble or hard times.

"Success grows in the soil of past failures and is watered by the deliberate, consistent and disciplined actions of those who pursue it."

Things will get tough and times will not always be pleasant but that does not mean you do not have to be unpleasant in your attitude. If you must cry, cry hard not long. If you must rest, rest well but not forever. If you must wait for your next move, wait patiently and strategize your next step. Never let a temporary event turn into a permanent regret.

> **"Discipline is the bridge between goals and accomplishments."**
> **–Jim Rohn**

Eventually your disciplines will become a delight when you see that your goals are being accomplished and your dreams being fulfilled. You have unquestionably heard someone say they wish they would having done this or wish that they could have done that. This becomes a sort of repetitive statement that most people say when they are too lazy, scarred or completely lost to the fact that wishes are only found in fairytales. If you want something, you must do something. Harry S. Truman said,

> **"In reading the lives of great men, I found that the first victory they won was over themselves; self-discipline with all of them came first."**

Be deliberate in your pursuit, consistent in your actions and discipline to keep moving forward regardless of what comes your way.

THE 6 INEVITABLE QUESTIONS

I am Disciplined enough to do what must be done to accomplish that which I want to achieve.

1. Who stops me from being disciplined?

2. What specific areas of my life do I need to apply discipline to?

3. When does discipline become a delight?

4. Where will my purpose (goal, destination, or objective) take me or allow me to do or have?

5. How will being disciplined in specific areas of my life help me to become successful?

6. Why is having discipline an important pillar to success?

Pillar Four:

PREPARE FOR OPPORTUNTIES

> **"Prepare thy work without, and make it fit for thyself in the field; and afterwards build thine house."**
> **Proverbs 24:27(KJV)**

Every day brings you a step closer. Every day you are being deliberate, every day you are being consistent, every day you are be discipline, prepares you and brings you that much closer to your dream, your goal, and the success you desire. Look at it like this, every day you have NOT YET achieved your desired outcome; when you are being deliberate, consistent, and disciplined it actually preparing you to receive that in which you want. Yes it may not have taken place, "yet", in your life. But know that it is happening. Earlier in Pillar One you read about what I call Intentional Progression: being on purpose, for purpose, with purpose. Well, the same is true in the preparing for opportunities. Except in this stage we do not just go through life, we grow through life by seizing opportunities and creating them for yourself.

SEIZE YOUR OPPORTUNITY

I will never forget working as a seasonal employee at Macy's in Atlanta. I was assigned to the children's department during the most busiest and chaotic seasons of the year: Christmas! While working there I would purposely come in dress in a conservative colored business suit and corresponding tie. I always made sure that I looked presentable and knew where everything was displayed and the sizes we had available. On this particular day, I was really not wanting to be there. I had just spent the prior eight hours in school and studying for some exams. When I came in I knew that it was going to be pretty busy, and for the next five and a half hours I was going to have to pull myself together so that I could properly get my work done. Our department was packed! People and children were everywhere. Clothes and displays were in disarray and each of the six registers had lines with five or more customers. To add to what appeared to be a hectic and stressful day, I was one of the three people who was not on the register, so that meant I had to start cleaning and rearranging the departmental floor.

I did not want to pick up clothes, fold clothes or fix displays just to find that someone else would soon come by and mess up what I just cleaned up. I remember walking out of our departmental office with a deep sigh thinking to myself, "I do not like folding clothes." As I walked over to the fist display, I ran into a disgruntled customer who had just dropped all her bags and in frustration exclaimed "I am done with all this shopping!" I pulled myself together and walked to pick up her bags and with a big smile I said, "You do not have to worry about carry another bag while you are in my store. I will not only hold your bags, I will help you finish your shopping and then check you out and the register." Her frown of frustration quickly turned into a smile of relief and we walked the department floor picking items to purchase for her grandchildren. When we got to the register I asked one of my co-workers to let me check her out and as I placed her items in the shopping bag, she stated, "I want to make you a manager." She handed me her card and I gave her the customary Macy's valediction while I placed her card in my pocket and did not think anything of her statement. There were many times I had customers give me their cards and ask me to work for them or with them, but none of the opportunities were to my liking.

At the end of the night as the store was closing, I pulled her card out of my pocket to read it. To my surprise the company name on the card said Macy's and the title listed under her name read: Senior Vice President. I was astonished and excited. I did not know that this woman worked for Macy's Corporate Office. I had no idea that she was who she was. I simply saw an opportunity to make someone feel better and make their shopping experience as pleasant as possible. Out of that one opportunity, so many doors were opened to me. I was promoted to manager, I was involved in new merchandising and product lines and even had the opportunity to do some modeling, all because I seized an opportunity.

DO YOU RECOGNIZE OPPORTUNITIES

Do you see the opportunities right in front of you? Are there better ways of doing things at work, school or church? Can you write a book or teach a lesson about a skillset that you know? Do you have a gift or idea that has helped you and know that other people will need it too?

You may say that you have no opportunities in your life. I would then say you are incorrect because you do have problems. Problems are opportunities in disguise. You must change the way you view problems.

"A pessimist sees the difficulty in every opportunity; an optimist sees the opportunity in every difficulty."
−Winston Churchill

The problems in your life will never go away until you fix them. You are the answer to solving the problems in your life. A message given by one of my mentors, Bishop Dale C. Bronner, entitled: *Good Perspective versus Wrong Perspective* tells of the "Six Right Perspectives Concerning Problems", they are as followed:

      1. Problems are unavoidable,
      2. Problems can be solved,
      3. Problems will pass,
      4. Problems make us better,
      5. Problems challenge us and
      6. Problems stretch us

After looking at those six points and you still can't see how problems are opportunities, you need to do some serious evaluation. Difficult times are necessary for a good performance and your problems become a platform on which you can stand and grow from. In the story of David versus Goliath, all the other Israelites could have faced Goliath if they chose to. Instead they saw a problem too big to face, and David saw an opportunity to big to miss. On your journey of success, you will have to use the acronym I call: P.O.W.E.R. Success and blessing always come disguised as **P**eople, **O**pportunities, **W**ork, **E**xperience, and **R**esponsibility. The issue is that many people do not want to use this P.O.W.E.R. and therefore miss out on their success. You must be willing to:

1. Deal with **PEOPLE**
2. Seize the **OPPORTUNITIES**
3. **WORK** for the success
4. Learn from **EXPERIENCES** and
5. Take **RESPONSIBILITY** for your actions.

You have an opportunity to help people who need help. You have the ability to locate opportunities in various setting by fixing the problems and meeting the needs around you. You have the opportunity to go above and beyond in the work you do to become the best in your field. If you did not know,

"The man who does more than he is paid for will soon be paid for more than he does."

−Napoleon Hill

You have the lessons from the experiences that you have learned from your past that can serve as an opportunity to help others not make the same mistakes you made. You have the opportunity to take responsibility for every area in your life leave no room for excuses.

ARE YOU PREPARED?

Are you prepared to reach your destination? Can you handle the success and all that comes with it? When As a business consultant, I meet with many business owners who want to grow and expand their business. One of the first questions I ask them during my evaluation of their needs is "Can you handle the growth that you want? And do you have the capacity to handle expansion?" This is not an easy question to answer. This requires you to take a deeper look and answer the following questions:

1. Where do you want to go?
2. Where are you in correspondence to question one?
3. Who are you? Does this fit into where you want to go? And
4. What do you currently have that can help you get to where you want to go?

If you noticed, these questions are similar to the "6 Inevitable Questions", but are a little more specific in their approach. If you are going to seize opportunities are you prepared to seize them? Are you positioned in the right place and doing the right things to get you where you want to go? Remember this:

"You do not get what you want in life you get what you prepare for."

Get meticulously tenacious with every location, step, and move you make. Live life as if it were so; live as if you are already where you want to be. You must not prepare for where you are now, but for where you are going. How much sense does it make to go to a basketball court and bring a baseball? Not much sense at all. Why? Because you are preparing to play basketball and not baseball. Oftentimes people say they are preparing to go somewhere in life but neglect to bring the proper equipment or really understand where it is they are going.

PREPARE FOR SUCCESS

One of the greatest signs that you believe in your desired outcome is shown in how you prepare for it. Preparation is tied to your pursuit. Another way we could say the first line is:

"The greatest proof that you desire something is found in how you pursue it."

I remember a family member of mine always wanted to go to Italy. She would talk about the trip, what she was going to do when she got there, and imagined being there taking in the sights. Not only did she talk and imagine the trip, she went and got new luggage, bought a brand new camera to take pictures and looked at the hotels she would stay at. Well, do you know, she was at a friend's house and they were packing getting ready to travel on a trip in two days. When asked where they were going, they replied to Italy. My family member exclaimed that she wanted to go and to her surprise her friends said that they had an extra ticket. The very thing that she was in pursuit of and preparing for took place. The point here is that you must prepare for what you want to see happen in your life. Make conscious efforts to go and do what needs to be done even before you see things happen. Practice the words of the Alexander Graham Bell:

"Before anything else, preparation is the key to success."

Prepare for that which you want to see happen, have and become in your life. Make every effort possible to be ready to handle the success you seek. Live your life as if you are already where you want to be and have the success you desire. Talk about it, read about it, pray about it, and study the skills or things needed in order to acquire it. Do all that you can with what you have, pursuing it tirelessly every day without quitting.

ATTRACT SUCCESS

Earlier you learned that the proof of desire is in your pursuit. As you pursue your dream, you are attracting the very thing you desire into your life. In Matthew 7:7 Jesus gives His listeners a perfect example of how our pursuits attract success. He says,

"Keep on asking and it will be given you; keep on seeking and you will find; keep on knocking and the door will be opened to you."
(AMP)

Do you see the parallel in each action? "Keep on…and it will be." If you keep on asking, seeking, and knocking; if you keep preparing yourself by doing what you have learned: deliberately, consistently, and being disciplined, it (whatever your dream, goal, destination, or desired outcome is) will be given to you; you will find and it will open up for you. Another way you could look at this is: you must ask for what you want, seek out what you asked for and knock on the doors of opportunity. When you do this, not quitting because nothing happened the first, second, third fourth or however many times prior, you will receive what you pursued.

The very thing that you desire is wanting you to find it. The success you seek is waiting to be found. The destination you are pursuing is ready for your arrival. As you begin to prepare and pursue opportunities, you will find that you do not have to pursue what you can attract. When you are continually deliberate, consistent, disciplined and in pursuit of your destination–opportunities that are align with that desire will begin to come on your path. Some opportunities will fall in your lap, others you will stumble upon on your proper path, and even more will begin to be an arm's reach away.

Even Jesus showed this truth when he stated to his disciples in John 14:2,

"...I go to prepare a place for you" (NKJV).

There is preparation to be done in order to receive what you desire. Just as much has the success if ready for you, you must be readily prepared for it.

YOU CAN ALWAYS DO SOMETHING

You may not have the money, resources, or even the skill set to do what you want to do or to accomplish what you can achieve. No matter if you have it or not, you do have the opportunity to prepare for what you want to see in your life. You can always do something. No matter how small, dumb, or crazy it may seem, you can do something that will bring you closer to your desired outcome. Robert Schuller said,

"It is never a lack of money, just ideas."

You are one idea, one thought, and one action away from seeing everything you want in your life to come to past. Remember that you must plan the work then work the plan. But I want to add a little more to that. You have to plan the work then work the plan, even if you don't have it in your hand.

"Take the first step in faith. You don't have to see the whole staircase. Just the first step."
−Dr. Martin Luther King Jr.

Look beyond your circumstances, look beyond what you don't have. There is always something in your hand. You have the idea, the hunger, and the clear decided choice of what you want. I remember there was a time in my life when I needed a vehicle. Anyone that lives in Atlanta knows that you have to have a car, because the transit system does not track over all the neighboring cities. So, before I even had the car or the money to get the vehicle, I started to look at what kind of car I wanted. After choosing the vehicle I wanted I started getting insurance quotes. When the insurance agent asked me the year and the model of the vehicle, I gave them the top three year models that I wanted the color and the mileage included. Not too long afterward; one month exactly, I got my new car. Many of us have goals and desires, but the truth of the matter is that we are not prepared to handle it.

We say we want it but do nothing to prepare for it. Would you give and infant a piece of steak? No! Why? Because thought that infant may smell the steak, cry about it and reach for it, they cannot handle it. That infant does not have teeth to properly consume the steak and thus if they tried it would only end up doing more harm than good. The same is true when it comes to your pursuit of success. Are you really prepared to handle all that you desire and seek after? Do you have the proper education, people, environment and integrity to handle what you are in pursuit of? If not it can be more harmful that good. And it is probably best that you have not obtained it at this moment so that you can prepare to have it.

Think of those individuals who have won millions of dollars playing the lottery and within a couple of years, they have spent it all and some end up broke and left worst off after the money than they were before they had it. These people had the desire to get money that is why they played the lottery. These people won a lot of money and now have the very thing they desired. In essence, they accomplished their goal but something was missing that caused them to end up back where they were or even worse. It is not they did not have money, or that they did not have the desire to win the money. The issue is in the fact that they were inadequately prepared to handle what was given to them. As a result, they lost it all and for some, their life is far worse than before they had the money. Just because you want it doesn't mean that you can handle. Actor Omar Epps profoundly stated it this way,

"I believe success is preparation, because opportunity is going to knock on your door sooner or later but are you

prepared to answer it [that]?"

You must prepare for the opportunities in your life. Opportunities are all around you, every day and come in many different ways. Are you prepared to handle them? Are you actively pursuing not only your destination but the preparation to handle the destination? Strive to become more, so that you can do more and eventually have more. Preparation is not only about the physical, but mental, emotional and spiritual capacity; which can help you not to squander everything you worked for.

Remember the greatest proof that you desire to succeed is in your preparation. Do not work so hard to pursue what you desire, only to lose it because you were not prepared for it.

THE 6 INEVITABLE QUESTIONS

I am Preparing for Opportunities by planning purposefully and prayerfully to count all my cost with consideration to what I want to achieve.

1. Who in my life can help me prepare for opportunities?

2. What opportunities do I want to seize?

3. When must I seize opportunities?

4. Where will these opportunities come from?

5. Based on what I have read thus far, how will I accomplish my purpose (goal, destination, or objective)?

6. Why is it important for me to seize opportunities if I want to be successful?

What Next:

YOUR MOVE

"Wealth is the product of man's capacity to think."
- Ayn Rand

Success is the Action of those thoughts. You must think like a man of action and act like a man of thought. You are responsible for the successes in your life or the lack there of.

GRAB EACH PILLAR

Pillars are tall vertical strong fortified structures used as a support for a building or monument; that are sturdy and able to withstand harsh conditions and inclement weather. This is why it is important for you to have these pillars in your life. Look at it this way,

> **"Anyone who listens to my teaching and follows it is wise, like a person who builds a house on solid rock. Though the rain comes in torrents and the floodwaters rise and the winds beat against, that house won't collapse because it is built on bedrock. But anyone who hears my teaching and doesn't obey it is foolish, like a person who builds a house on sand. When the rains and floods come the winds beat against that house, it will collapse with a mighty crash."**
> **—Matthew 7:24-27 (NLT)**

You have read what it takes to obtain, sustain, and regain success. Nevertheless as always, it is up to you. You must apply what you have read and make a strong foundation for your life in order to see what you desire to come to past. The beauty of this scripture is that no matter if you listen and apply the pillars into your life, you will eventually face rains and floods (tests, trials, and obstacles). The only difference is that if you are serious about reaching your destination and becoming successful, you will make the effort and apply what you have read. Action is the beginning of everything. Breaking ground on the first level is the hardest, but after that you can grow with ease.

SUCCESS IS SIMPLE, NOT EASY

Success is not a destination or even a particular

accomplishment. Success is really maximizing what you have been given and doing the best with what you have. What is doing the best? It is doing all that you can do within your given ability and opportunity to learn to do, to make the most of what you have been given. Success is simple, not easy. It is simple to follow these steps to reach your destination, accomplish your goals and make your dreams a reality. However applying these steps (See Pillar Two) is not easy. It is not easy because you have to fight against daily hindrances and unforeseen variables like the death of a love one, a break-up, a lay-off, an illness or a myriad of other things you did not anticipate or see coming and you have no control over.

Some may ask, "What if I do not have the information or knowledge to pursue my desired outcome?" My response to them would be that it is up to you to go and get what you need for the journey. Hosea 4:6 states,

"My people are destroyed for lack of knowledge…"

If you do not know you cannot sow, and you cannot grow. In today's society, information is a mouse-click away. You can find resources all over the internet and learn from people from all over the world. Not knowing and not doing is no longer an adequate excuse, and frankly put, it never was.

A Little Something Extra:

IT'S SIMPLE

> **"Success is simple, not easy."**
> **- Stephen J. Palmer**

Again I say: It is simple to follow these steps, but it is not easy to apply them to your life. Why? Because you are faced with a cluster of variables and distractions that fight against your progress. You may have to deal with the death of a love one, a break-up, a layoff, an illness or a myriad of other things that you did not see coming and most which you do not have control over. Part of living is experiencing the ups and downs; the positive and negatives; the good and not so good.

You have to learn to dance in the sun and sing in the rain.

You must learn to brace yourself for the things that may come and determine in your mind that you will not allow them to stop you. Your emotions and feeling can get in the way, your physical body will not want to adjust, the negative thoughts and questions such as, "is this really working" plague your mind; and you look right at the immediate problems in your life and wonder if it will ever get any better. Success requires you to work. However, after reading this book I am sure you are ready to do the work necessary to reach your desired outcome.

WITHIN YOU

Within you lay the greatest potential, substance, and treasures of your life that uniquely and clearly belong to you. For some this treasure lays dormant unknown, undiscovered, and never realized and allowed to be revealed. For others that have started their search for success and a quest for bettering themselves and the world in which we live; the digging processes has begun; awakening this treasure through glimpses of light and fetal matter. Each treasure is your own. Though it may be shared, it can never be counted, collected and stored away in a safe, bank, or in a mattress. It belongs to you and it is you. It is your essence, your power, your gift and the measure that you will use to obtain the success you seek. In your pursuit for success, never forget that success is what you make of it and that each internal decision determines your external reward.

Within you is the substance of things hoped for. The essence of things unseen (Hebrews 11). Liken to a chemist mixing a combination of chemicals you must take the substance you have and mix it with the four pillars and watch and the metamorphosis and a change reaction begins to take place. You are the catalyst, the change agent. You are the treasure; you are the success you seek. And you must find it. Proverbs 25:2 says,

"It is the glory of God to conceal a matter, but the glory of kings is to search out a matter." (NASB)

You become a king when you search out the hidden matter–your internal treasure to help you achieve your desired outcome [success]. You do not become great by living an undiscovered you. You become great by discovering what it is you seek. And like many explorers, as you begin to search out the treasures within, you will stumble across many valuable truths and new discoveries in and of themselves concerning your life and the desired success you seek. You will be transformed and become the success. Therefore, continue to be deliberate, consistent, disciplined, and prepare for the opportunities you seek. For just as you desire to seek them out, they desire to be found by you.

SHARE YOUR LIGHT

The destination is not as important as what you become. I know that throughout this book we have talked about accomplishing a goal, reaching a destination or making a dream a reality. The important thing is not just where you go but who you become. Your dream should be so big and so grand, that you cannot achieve it without becoming the person who can handle it. You become the very quintessence of what you pursue. Make it a goal to be better in every area of your life. Do not just pursue a destination or a tangible object. Strive to make the light that shines within you burn so bright that you inspire others to do the same.

ABOUT THE AUTHOR

Stephen is an experienced enterpriser turned author and speaker with an outstanding track record best described as "getting the job done." His previous leadership roles range from corporate manager, law enforcement professional to church youth leader. His rare experiences and ability to relate personably with his audience make his books and his appearance a 'must-have' for your next event. His thought provoking, humorous and uniquely tailored messages "generate ideas and initiate action" to his wide variety of audiences. He creatively takes a hands on approach through audience participation and various analogies that is sure to inspire all those who read and hear him speak.

"Be Bold, Be Daring, Be Life-Changing!"
—Stephen J. Palmer

Made in the USA
Columbia, SC
21 July 2023